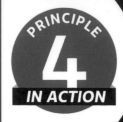

PRINCIPLE 4 IN ACTION

ADAPT LESSON DELIVERY AS NEEDED

Being able to adjust based on students' experiences in an online class is even more important than in face-to-face instruction. Whether students can persevere and ultimately succeed depends in large part on how the teacher is able to accommodate them.

> *Unlike a traditional classroom, distance learning is easy to leave and difficult to rejoin after a period of absence. The most essential role for the teacher is to keep students coming.*

Quick Tips

Support participation

- Notice what is happening to individual students in the class.
  - ☐ Are they logging in?
  - ☐ Are they present for live sessions?
  - ☐ Are they submitting tasks on time?
  - ☐ Do they contact you when they need help?
  - ☐ Is the mode of instruction working for them?
- Hold one-on-one support sessions weekly to gain a better understanding and to explore solutions.
- Attend to social and emotional needs and technical problems.
- Connect students with paraprofessionals or bilingual social workers.

Differentiate instruction for individual learners

- As you monitor each student's performance, you may realize that some need supplementary materials or instruction that relates to their cultural and linguistic background.
- Allow students to respond on the levels that they can perform independently, including the option to complete some tasks in the home language. They may not have an adult's help that you had anticipated for the task.
- Add in as-needed teaching in breakout groups or invite students to practice or to extracurricular sessions.
- Be flexible with pacing. Let students slow down or complete fewer/ differentiated tasks.
- Give prompt feedback that considers the whole child and helps them put forth their best effort.

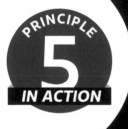

PRINCIPLE 5 IN ACTION

MONITOR AND ASSESS STUDENT LANGUAGE DEVELOPMENT

Regularly monitoring our students' language performance helps to gauge how they are progressing toward proficiency. This is harder to do in remote teaching because we cannot always tell how independently students worked and what supports they used to produce a piece of writing, comprehend a text, or record a video. Although sometimes less reliable for measuring language growth, assessments are still very important in remote teaching for motivating students to engage with the content and show learning outcomes.

> *I meet with students in small groups daily via videoconferencing. We start with a morning meeting for social and emotional support in the form of a connection activity or game. After this structured social opportunity, I guide them through the lesson objectives and learning tasks for the day. I model for them what they will be doing and help them get started with their tasks. After I release the group, I am able to monitor what each student has completed and add my feedback either in video or text. In the afternoon, I send invitations for one-on-one tutoring or small group conferencing based on the work that each student has submitted. I make phone calls home weekly to check on wellness and to communicate about students' progress.*

Quick Tips

Select the kinds of formative assessments that lead to skills practice and engagement with the course material

- Spur some learning action with a well-placed quiz, a quick contest, or the desire to earn a micro badge (e.g., with the Kahoot! app).
- Motivate students to do good work by giving them a virtual forum to display their work and to give each other feedback (e.g., Flipgrid or similar programs).
- Have students create practice quizzes for themselves and their classmates (e.g., using Quizlet).
- Give students the opportunity to share their best creations in a portfolio (e.g., in Seesaw).

Collect and analyze student data over time

- Decide on the assignments that best reflect students' progress over time. Focus on just a few routine performance tasks that you can track (e.g., book review presentations, journal entries, or videotaped comments to prompts on Seesaw or Flipgrid).
- Sample these tasks regularly for elements of growth with academic language skills in listening, speaking, reading, and writing.
- Treat language errors as a natural part of development and study them for language features that students are ready to learn next.
- Review the assessment data available to you in the web-based adaptive curriculum packages that your students are working on (e.g., Imagine Learning, i-Ready, Learning A-Z, Lexia, or MobyMax).
- Use assessment data to adjust instruction: Add more practice, fill learning gaps to move students up the proficiency scale, schedule reteaching time with a small group.

PRINCIPLE 6 IN ACTION

ENGAGE AND COLLABORATE WITHIN A COMMUNITY OF PRACTICE

The effective way to serve your English learners is to coordinate their content learning and language support with all of their teachers. When you plan and teach as a team with a unified approach to providing supports to each learner, students can exercise their language skills in every class, which reduces the time to master academic language skills.

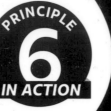

> *I try to link remote learning to what we have done in classroom instruction. We use the same learning management system and the same web-based instructional programs. The familiarity helps students feel comfortable and the routine eases the learning curve. We use the same social media group to publish our work. I have recorded myself reading multicultural books to my students, which I do often in face-to-face instruction. I send weekly "check-in" texts to English learner families using the TalkingPoints app and handwritten letters to each of my students.*

Quick Tips

Collaborate with a school team regularly

- Scheduled meetings with the teachers and staff who serve English learners are even more important when informal face-to-face meetings don't occur naturally.
- Reduce the barriers to technology by simplifying and streamlining your courses; agree with other teachers to use the same platforms and tools.
- Follow the performance of individual English learners to assure that their support is congruent from one teacher's class to another.
- Monitor recently exited students more regularly than typically done.
- Exchange strategies that have worked and explore solutions together, keeping a positive can-do approach. Your collective expertise and shared advocacy for each English learner will surpass whatever you can accomplish individually.

Seek professional learning from a supportive group

- Remote teaching with technology can be intimidating at first; if you are a novice at it, don't be shy to admit that you have learning to do. Find a good coach who is experienced with English learners and who shares your commitment to their success.
- Join a professional organization, like TESOL, whose members and activities center on supporting the teachers of English learners and can provide you with a direct line to best practices.
- Draw on the resources available to you through your state's migrant education and English learner programs and other federally funded initiatives dedicated to improving the education of English learners.
- Utilize high-quality lessons from resource collections that address remote teaching, and contribute to these collections as well.

Reference: U.S. Department of Education. (2018). *National Study of English Learners and Digital Learning Resources: Developer toolkit. Creating educational technology for English learners.*

More 6 Principles Resources

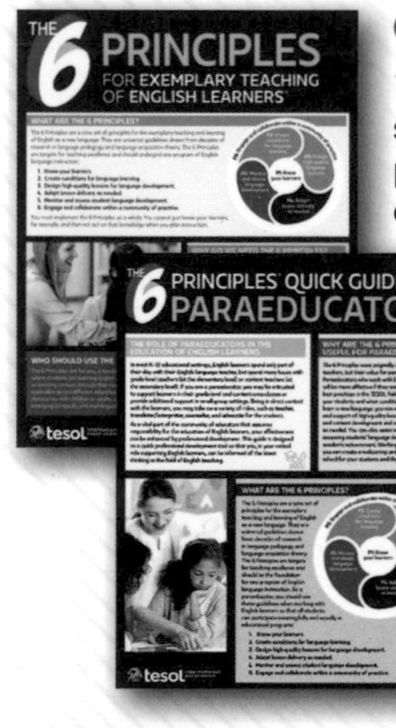

QUICK GUIDES

The 6 Principles® Quick Guides showcase easy-to-use, research-based practices for the exemplary teaching of English learners in a variety of settings. Written by English language teaching experts, these tips, checklists, and teaching techniques are handy tools to ensure your lessons incorporate current knowledge on second language learning and pedagogy. Your students will experience success as they develop their English language skills.

COMING SOON *The 6 Principles Quick Guide for Grades K–12,* Andrea B. Hellman

BOOKS

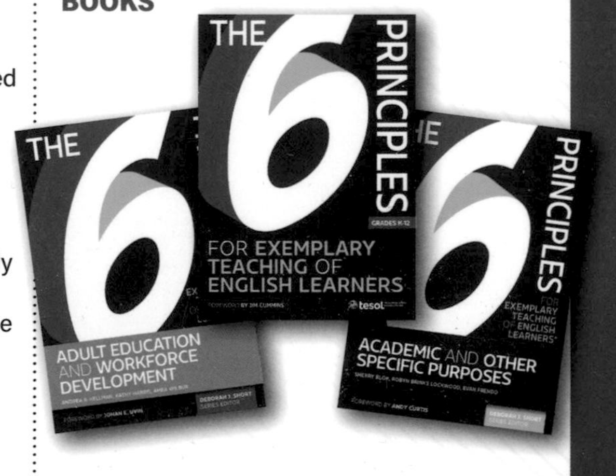

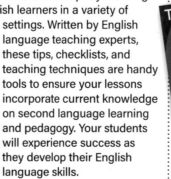

COMING SOON *The 6 Principles for Exemplary Teaching of English Learners: Young Learners,* Joan Shin, Vera Savić, Tomohisa Machida

SAVE 10% when you buy in packs of 25! Great for workshops and PLCs.
For more information on The 6 Principles, visit www.the6principles.org.

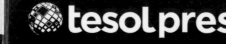

ABOUT THE AUTHOR

Andrea B. Hellman, EdD, is a lifelong TESOL educator. She directs a National Professional Development project for in-service teachers at Missouri State University, where she is an associate professor.

ISBN 978-1-942799-83-2

9 781942 799832

TESOL Press Product ID# 14158 (single); 14160 (25-pack)

tesolpress

© 2021 TESOL International Association. All rights reserved. Not for reproduction.

THE 6 PRINCIPLES®

Quick Guide

Remote Teaching of K-12 English Learners

WHAT ARE THE 6 PRINCIPLES?

TESOL International Association's *The 6 Principles® for the Exemplary Teaching of English Learners* are a core set of principles for the exemplary teaching and learning of English as a new language. They are universal guidelines drawn from decades of research in language pedagogy and language acquisition theory.

The 6 Principles are targets for teaching excellence and should be the foundation for any program of English language instruction:

1. **Know your learners.**
2. **Create conditions for language learning.**
3. **Design high-quality lessons for language development.**
4. **Adapt lesson delivery as needed.**
5. **Monitor and assess student language development.**
6. **Engage and collaborate within a community of practice.**

Although remote teaching of English learners is fairly new to K–12 educators, The 6 Principles offer relevant guidelines for this mode of instruction. Even at a distance, we can design and deliver lessons that engage our students and promote their educational success.

REMOTE TEACHING *for English learners is...*

- ADVOCATING FOR **EQUITY & ACCESS**
- **GIVING VOICE** *to English learner families during planning*
- **PREPARING CAREGIVERS** *for their* **NEW ROLES**
- *Supplying the* **TOOLS** *of* **LEARNING**
- *Caring for* **SOCIOEMOTIONAL NEEDS**
- REACHING OUT TO **vulnerable students**
- Tapping home **RESOURCES**
- *Reaching for* **TRIED-AND-TRUE** *methods*
- **Boosting PARTICIPATION**
- FINDING **solutions that work** FOR FAMILIES

PUTTING THE 6 PRINCIPLES INTO ACTION

This Quick Guide is a planning tool and practical framework for action based on The 6 Principles; it is for English learner specialists, English language development teachers, classroom teachers of English learners, school staff, and school leaders who are planning and implementing remote instruction for their students. Teams of educators can use this Quick Guide to develop unified remote teaching plans that can ensure English learners' access to a meaningful education.

tesolpress

T0124026

PRINCIPLE 1 IN ACTION

KNOW YOUR LEARNERS

The families of English learners are the most diverse groups in schools. Though some have the skills and resources to participate in remote teaching, the majority will need comprehensive supports.

Quick Tips

✔ Communicate with the families of English learners directly

- Invest the necessary effort to make meaningful contact with every family.
- Form a positive relationship early and communicate weekly about the children's engagement in learning.
- Utilize parent liaisons, paraprofessionals, translators, interpreters, and translation software for two-way communication with caregivers.
- Update contact information regularly to have multiple ways to reach each family/caregiver. Recognize that some families move during difficult times.

✔ Assess families' readiness for online learning

Interview caregivers with an interpreter or send a survey in their preferred language and offer assistance to complete it. *Add to these survey items as appropriate:*

- Can your child access the internet at home?
- Is your internet service sufficient to serve multiple devices at the same time?
- Do you plan to borrow a device [tablet/laptop computer/hotspot for internet access] from school?
- We can provide options for schoolwork. Select what works for you.
- A teacher will update you on your student's schoolwork. Choose how you want to connect with teachers.
- Please watch our videos for parents at [insert link].
- Do you have more questions that we can answer?

✔ Keep administrators informed of what families prefer and how families can overcome barriers to participation

What can the district do?

- Involve caregivers in the planning of remote teaching.
- Adopt policies that promote equity and access for English learners.
- Improve the effectiveness of the district's communication strategies for English learner families.
- Provide training to teachers on the available interpretation and translation services.
- Dedicate resources to reach and mentor English learner families. (E.g., hire a bilingual family liaison and home-learning coaches.)
- Lend equipment to students.
- Form community partnerships with internet providers and libraries.
- Provide a multilingual technology hotline.
- Establish satellite learning sites and tutoring services at community organizations that serve English learner families.
- Make available a list of community sites with internet access.
- Implement a safety protocol that enables school staff to visit with families when needed.

> *We have to be careful that with remote learning, we aren't thrusting the caregivers of English learners into the role of an untrained teacher, expecting them to use tools that we have selected for them but not with them and requiring them to commit time to this role that they don't have.*

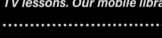

> *I rode the school bus to deliver learning packets to families. A mom with a baby was looking after the children of several working families in a bustling home. She did not have the capacity to direct the children's study individually. Fortunately, our district offers instructional television on a daily schedule. We can supply the materials that the TV teacher uses in the lessons and we can bring families learning games that were specifically designed for multi-age groups to play together to practice the concepts taught in the TV lessons. Our mobile library circulates bilingual and recorded books, as well as DVDs of instructional TV lessons.*

PRINCIPLE 2 IN ACTION

CREATE CONDITIONS FOR LANGUAGE LEARNING

Remote teaching is also home learning. Before we transfer responsibilities to caregivers for instructing their children with the tools and materials that educators have selected, we should ensure that caregivers are willing and able to perform those roles.

Quick Tips

✔ Design the approach for access

What is the best approach for your students?

Before you decide, consider not only the technology required but also the time commitment expected from caregivers to guide their children with the materials. Be sure to develop and post videos for students and caregivers on how to use online learning platforms.

✔ Reflect on the design from the families' perspective

- ✔ Do they have the technology and supplies needed?
- ✔ How will the caregivers get prepared for their responsibilities?
- ✔ How are languages used in the home?
- ✔ How many children are being schooled and what ages are they?

> *We have created a virtual resource room for our multilingual families. They can access a library of videos about the features of our district's digital learning for each grade. Three times a week, parents can join a live video conference with a teacher, where they have simultaneous interpretation.*

Chart: Technology in the home

Vertical axis: Commitment from caregiver (HIGH to LOW)
Horizontal axis: Technology in the home (MORE ACCESS to LESS ACCESS)

Items plotted:
- Textbooks, Workbooks, Printed activity packets
- Asynchronous online learning
- Printable materials
- Web-based adaptive curriculum packages
- Synchronous online learning
- Instructional television
- Mobile learning apps
- Webinars, Video lessons

Horizontal axis labels: No technology | Television | Smartphone | Quality device, Basic internet | Computer, Printer with ink | Quality device, Fast internet

---

✔ Select tools that suit your students

You can reduce stress and prevent problems by carefully choosing your digital tools from the start. Opt for tools that are the least likely to create obstacles for students or their families. Rather than experimenting with the latest, you can focus on the quality of content delivered with technology that everyone can operate competently. Limit the total number of different tools depending on the age and proficiency level of students.

Apply these criteria for picking the right digital tools:

- Students have already learned to use the tool independently.
- Students can log in and access the tool from home.
- The tool is easy to manipulate and manage with the input devices students have (e.g., touchpad, touchscreen, mouse, keyboard, camera, and microphone).
- The tool suits the internet service families can afford (for time online, speed, the number of different internet users, and cost).
- Caregivers know how to minimize any potential safety issues, and they consent to use.
- Tutorials are available to help caregivers assist learners.
- Technology help is provided for troubleshooting problems with the tool.
- Teachers can monitor students' use of the tool and have an easy way to comment on their performance.
- Learners sustain productive use of the tool over time.

✔ Organize learning to be simple and consistent

- Develop routines for distance learning and teach these explicitly.
- Reduce the number of programs, platforms, websites, and apps.
- On the learning management system, organize and label everything clearly. Remove links to tools that you will not be using.
- For all files, materials, and links that you provide, add clear task explanations for what you expect students to do with them. Do not assume they are using a tool or materials just because you have made them available.
- Chunk instruction into small, manageable units that students can complete in one session.

✔ Teach how to be a successful student

- Communicate norms for attendance, participation, work ethic, and due dates.
- Hold all students to high expectations while being nimble with necessary accommodations.
- Practice with students the use of the tools that you have provided.
- Demonstrate learning strategies and have students exchange strategies that are working for them.
- Explain when and how to ask for help with the lesson tasks.

Prepare everyone for their tasks

Here is what to get ready.

Teachers have:

- ☐ Updated caregiver contact info
- ☐ Preferred communication strategy for each family
- ☐ Students' login information for learning platforms
- ☐ Interpreters and translators for home languages
- ☐ Quality content materials for learning in digital form
- ☐ Quality alternate method to digital learning
- ☐ Weekly and daily schedule for students

Students can:

- ☐ Log in and use their learning platform and apps
- ☐ Solve basic technical problems or know how to get help with these
- ☐ Contact their teachers with questions

Caregivers know:

- ☐ How to protect students' safety online
- ☐ How to borrow devices from school
- ☐ How to access affordable internet service
- ☐ Where to get help with technology
- ☐ Where to find comprehensible information from the school about the available services
- ☐ How to reach each child's teachers
- ☐ How to support learning at home
- ☐ How to use the alternate method offered for home learning

👁 Watch and learn

Houston Independent School District @H.O.M.E. TV (blogs.houstonisd.org/hisdtv)

Let's Learn NYC! (www.thirteen.org/programs/lets-learn-nyc)

PBS Learning Media (pbslearningmedia.org)

Annenberg Learner (www.learner.org)

PRINCIPLE 3 IN ACTION

DESIGN HIGH-QUALITY LESSONS FOR LANGUAGE DEVELOPMENT

High-quality lessons form an organized instructional path that follows grade-level standards. Students hone their academic language skills with listening, speaking, reading, and writing while they are actively engaging with content that holds meaning for them. They have ample opportunities to apply their new knowledge and to practice their new skills to develop mastery and become self-regulated learners.

Quick Tips

✔ Apply criteria for selecting digital content

Creating successful instruction for online delivery is different from replicating face-to-face lessons. Some teaching activities—like teacher presentations—are easier to reproduce, but still they take much time and preparation. A more efficient approach is to curate available digital content and to focus on clear delivery and students' active engagement with those materials.

Many teachers use a basic digital lesson format and select digital content (images, audio, videos, readings, learning games) to fit within that format.

✔ Embed digital support features that scaffold comprehension for English learners

Following the findings of a national study in the United States (U.S. Department of Education, 2018), developers have been adding features to their digital content that can aid English language learning. When students know how to utilize these, they can access texts and presentations that had previously been beyond their independent level of learning.

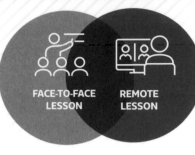

FACE-TO-FACE LESSON / REMOTE LESSON

What elements of high-quality lessons for English learners are found both in face-to-face and remote instruction?

- ☐ Students focus on clear lesson objectives.
- ☐ The lesson objectives include both content and language learning targets.
- ☐ The content and the activities are meaningful to students' lives.
- ☐ Students build on their existing knowledge and prior learning.
- ☐ The materials are clear and comprehensible on the students' level.
- ☐ Students actively engage—body and mind—with the content by reading it, talking and writing about it, and creating with it.
- ☐ The pacing allows for processing and practicing both the content and the language of the content.
- ☐ Students gain strategies that help them experience success.
- ☐ Teachers give students feedback on their language use and content learning.
- ☐ Teachers assess student progress on lesson objectives.

🖱 How to use a digital lesson template

Focus question or image to cue lesson topic: [insert interesting image] 1 >	**Prompt to activate prior knowledge:** Talk, write, or draw what you already know. 2 >	**Learning objectives:** [insert learner-friendly content and language objective] 3 >	**Prompt to process objectives:** Say in your own words what you will take away from this lesson. 4 >
Activities to do to achieve the lesson objectives: [insert list of activities] 5 >	**Key words introduction:** [insert content vocabulary and general academic words] 6 >	**Key words demonstration:** [insert pronunciation/illustration/examples/use of key words] 7 >	**Prompt for key words:** Read and use these words. 8 >
Watch a short video: [embed link to video] 9 >	**Prompt to respond to the video:** [insert link to a technology tool, like VoiceThread or EdPuzzle] 10 >	**Choose a text to read:** [embed links to texts on different reading levels] 11 >	**Prompt to engage with the text:** [insert link to discussion board] 12 >
Practice activity or project creation: [link to a project tool, like Genially] 13 >	**Summary of learning:** 14 >	**Review of new words encountered:** 15 >	**Review of the lesson objectives:** 16 >
Prompt for assessment task: [link to quiz, survey, or exit ticket] 17 >			

👁 See example lessons

Florida Virtual School (tinyurl.com/y6p47jf4)

Teaching Matters (teachingmatters.org/learning-from-home)

Digital support features to look for

In video: closed captioning, transcript, translation, spoken translation, voice/video comments

In text: read-aloud, translation, larger font, illustrations, link to picture/spoken dictionary, link to easy definition/glossary, highlighted words, annotation tool, guiding questions, comprehension questions

See digital support features at work

CommonLit (www.commonlit.org/en)

ReadWorks (www.readworks.org)

> *Some students will click through the course content mindlessly, thinking they have done what was required of them. Unless they have a purpose for learning, they might choose the easy route "to be done." It's important to have creative tools for them so they can interact with each other, sharing the products of their learning.*